CARING FOR YOUR MARK ONE FEMALE ANDROID

A DETAILED SERVICE MANUAL

PREPARED BY THE DESIGN TEAM
AND

MIKE RILEY

THIS BOOK IS DEDICATED TO
KAREN RILEY, MY WIFE,
THE INSPIRATION FOR THE MARK ONE FEMALE
AND WITHOUT HER I WOULD NEED
AN ACTUAL REAL MARK ONE.

INTRODUCTION

Congratulations on your purchase of a brand new Mark One Female Help-mate android! You are now on the leading edge of a brave new world! You could not have made a better choice to maximize your happiness.

Ten years ago, at the dawn of time so to speak, our company created a survey of the happiness coefficient of human male and females in human relationships. It was an exhaustive survey including almost 15 subjects. It found that women often subtracted happiness from the male rather than adding to the relationship. From that remarkable finding, the seed of the Mark One was created.

Your Help-mate was created to maximize the male happiness; your happiness! Anything that the human woman can do, the Mark One can do better! With proper Modules installed, the Mark One is not only a Cordon Bleu chef but also a Cordon Rouge! On a rating system of one to ten, a survey of almost 10 men judged the Mark One to be an 11 as a lover both in bed and out of it. Your Mark One will keep your house in perfect order, your car shined, your lawn mowed and even your golf clubs cleaned, all with a smile on her face and a song in her 'heart.'

The Help-mates patented Docking System insures that the Mark One is always charged up, tuned up and raring to go, all without any help from you! At any time your Help-mate can be serving you a meal worthy of the world's great hotels, all while massaging your neck and shining your shoes!   At the slightest request, your Mark One is eager to jump into bed to service your every desire.   And will thank you afterwards.

All your needs will be taken care of in the peace and tranquility of the Help-mate experience!   Not only that! Your Mark One comes with the famous Pleasure Program included at no extra charge. Think of it. You Mark One has the memories and abilities of every famed seductress from Cleopatra to Marilyn Monroe, from Sophia Loren to Taylor Swift!   With the Pleasure Program's new and improved Control Panel, you are in charge. You can tailor your sexual needs to your complete satisfaction.   Money back guarantee!*

Your children's school work will get better as will your wife's mood. The Mark One not only does your wife's chores but keeps her happy as well.

In the social world of humans, a man might spend most of his life seeking the perfect wife. This is no longer needed. Visit our factory and experience the joy and power of a Mark One Female.   While it may not be love at first sight, we guarantee that the user will come to prefer his Mark One over any of the bar fodder he is accustomed to dating. Not only is she perfectly obedient, helpful, sexy, undemanding, more than willing, and if you don't like some aspect of her personality, a simple sub-routine installation will change her into the girl of your dreams! Why are you wasting your money down at the bars? Come visit the Mark One factories and see your perfect help mate! Forget your dreams, your reality is just a few bucks away!

You were one smart man when you bought your Mark One!

*(certain restrictions apply)

COMMANDS

All commands must be given to the Mark One Female Help-mate in the right format or the result will be erratic. Unfortunately the format changes with the program the female is running at the time. If the female is running a Pleasure Program, proper commands are especially important.

Your female has been designed to respond to verbal commands, however the tone of your voice while giving the command must be in the proper correlation to the command. This is a bug that we of the Design Team are struggling to eradicate. As of this time, however, tone is an important component of your female.

If, for example, your female is in the pleasure mode, you give her a command with your nose in the air while gazing at her as a superior, the results of your command will be erratic and most often will result in a crash of the Pleasure Program. This is confusing as the same tone used while your female is in a Lecture Program will be recognized as a proper command.

Another bug we of the Design Team are struggling with is removing the remnants of an old recognition program from an older female series. For example if you are instructing your female to go to the store and buy certain items, the program will crash unless you include a meeting of the lips and an archaic phrase, "I love you." We realize that one is unsanitary and the other meaningless outside of a Pleasure Program. Please keep in mind that your female is a complicated device and many of the programs are still in beta. The end result, if the above actions are not taken in an Instructing Program, is the program will crash and your female will refuse to go to the store and most likely will go to get her hair done instead.

COMPATIBILITY

Every effort is made to create females that will be compatible to a wide range of users, however if you require special behaviors from your female, you should approach the Design Team before purchasing your unit. Many special chips are available for upgrading your unit as it is recognized that each user is a unique individual.

In a normal control box instructions, you will notice many slide bars for adjusting various behaviors. Below the slide bar is a box which if checked will turn off the behavior. For example, notice the slide bar for sexual behavior. The bar starts at nymphomaniac, followed by whore, wanton, slutty, average, Saturday night only, chaste and virginal. Notice the advance bar, clicking this will bring you to a sub screen where you check those preferences you prefer. These run from missionary, doggy, on top, oral, anal, other females and lastly to orgy. Be aware that you can always reset your female to default selections by clicking the default button on the main control bar as we realize that you may wish that your female revert to a previous behavior after the orgy option.

Because you have purchased A Mark One Female Help-mate, her control panel has been relocated within her main frame and is now accessed by adjusting various parts of her anatomy. More information can be found in the Control Panel Section. The various options for sexual pleasure remain the same.

Your female has also been designed to change compatibility functions with voice activation. This will require practice by you, the user. The voice command must be phrased exactly or it will not be recognized as a proper command by your female. For example, if you wish your female to perform a doggy style program, you must give the command:

"It will make my cock feel so large inside of you."

It is recognized that the above command makes no sense to the user as we all know that the female has been designed to conform her lower Pleasure Center to perfectly fit any size user. Unfortunately, it should be noted that the female, thru a virus that escaped our detection, has come to prefer larger endowed users.

If your female laughs when viewing your sexual organs, your female has picked up the dreaded 'Sarcastic Virus.' Deletion of this virus is difficult but since your female will be all but useless unless it is eradicated. The longer the 'Sarcastic Virus' is active, the more files and programs it will infect. In time the virus will take over your entire female and you will have no choice but to replace your female through an expensive and difficult procedure. If your female shows signs of this extremely dangerous virus, contact your Design Team immediately who will repair your female for a minor additional cost.

The behavior of your female can be adjusted to fit the needs of each individual user. Some users prefer a more dominating female, others a more compliant Help-mate. Be sure to discuss these options with your sales team before leaving the store with your purchase. Interesting behaviors that the user might consider installing into his female are: Clothing Adverse, Yoga Enabled (for more exciting positions), Objectafilia (Urge for objects to be inserted into certain parts of her body), Orally Fixated and Orgy Fixated. These options are often more difficult to remove than to install. Be sure you really want the behavior for your female before you ask for it to be installed.

Basic appearance of your female can be adjusted at a Design Team sanctioned Beauty Parlor. Items such as hair color, nail length and color, and skin tone can be done within a few hours. Other options such as breast size, permanent eye color, throat and tongue length and tightness of the vagina require a visit to the factory, but can be completed within a week.

We, at Mark One Females, want your Help-mate experience to be life altering. We are willing to do whatever you want within reason, please don't hesitate to inquire.

CONTROL PANEL

Every effort has been made to make your female seem as realistic as possible. For this reason her control panel has been redesigned and the female's controls placed all over her body. For example, to start the Pleasure Program hold both of her breasts in your hands from behind while placing your lips upon her neck. Instead of sliding controls to select the degree of intensity of the Pleasure Program, the following controls have been placed on the female's body to be used in a Pleasure Program only.

Slide Control	Program Response Intensity
Nibble on right ear	Chaste
Nibble on left ear	Saturday Night Only
Whisper "I Love You."	Virginal
Squeeze Breasts	Average
Insert tongue in ear	Slutty
Squeeze nipples	Wanton
Bite nipples	Whore
Insert finger in vagina	Repeated wifely duty
Rub clitoris	Nymphomaniac

To adjust the above behaviors, note the advanced options. Access the advanced options by pulling the small hairs on the back of her neck while sucking the hollow at the base of her throat.

Advanced Options	Program Response Choice
Insert tongue in mouth	Missionary Style
Rub buttocks	Doggie Style
Scratch scalp	Female On Top Style
Place ring on finger	Oral Style
Spank buttocks	Anal Style
Lick clitoris	Females Together Style
Insert Dildo into vagina	Orgy Style

New Controls can always being added to your female. Every effort is made to keep you informed of new corrections and upcoming models, but to be sure of being fully informed, contact your Mark One Help-mate's web site at monthly intervals.

If you have a different option in mind, please let us know. Many users require different options ranging from S and M, sharpened teeth, raspy tongues, and a clitoris that enlarges to the size of a male organ. Specialized controls can be added to your Mark One for a fairly minor additional cost.

If you have problems with accessing some of the options of the Control Panel, before you return your female, you may access the Control Panel through a USB port deep within the female's belly button. As an aside, this USB port is also useful for charging your cell phone.

(Additionally fees can exceed 1.5 times the original unit cost)

RESTART

Any digital tool that runs on software can become confused. That is an anthropomorphic statement. Sorry. It is normal to make such mistakes. The Mark One Help-mate is so human-like that it is easy to describe her as a human. However she isn't.

Humans rely on an organic brain which, when it is working up to specs, is a marvel of evolutionary engineering. One problem is it is subject to chemical imbalance. Given enough chemicals, especially psychotic inducing substances like LSD, heroin, acid, angel dust, star sprinkle and even marijuana, the human brain will stop functioning or at the best, give erratic solutions to important problems such as recognizing whether the light is red or green..

The Mark One Female can ingest any number of psychotic chemicals with out harm to its CPU. That does not mean that it is fool proof. Any android type computer, of which the Mark One is an example, is subject to conflicting programs hogging CPU time. When several or more programs are sharing CPU time, parts of their programs that are superficially alike can be pirated by another program. When this happens the Mark One can start to act erratically. The easiest solution for this problem is to restart the unit.

Realizing that restarts might become important due to the increasing number of programs that can be run in the Mark One, the Design Team made restarting easy and fun. Simply kiss the Mark One and insert your tongue underneath the

Mark One's tongue, anywhere is fine and the restart will begin. Don't remove your tongue. The Mark One will restart in milliseconds and your kiss will assure that the Mark One will restart in the Pleasure Program. This is the Mark One's primary program. Anthropomorphically speaking, when the Mark One is running her Pleasure Program she is as happy as an android can be.

If you restart your Mark One and then instantly withdraw your tongue, the Help-mate will restart and run any program it feels is appropriate at the time. Since you will still be in her face, staring at her, and the sensation of the kiss will still be in her mouth, chances are she will restart in a Bitch Program. Why this is so is unknown at this time. Usually her first response is one of the following:

>"What do you think you were doing?"

>"Get the f___ out of my face."

>"Who let you out of the zoo?

Remember that the default for exiting the Bitch Program is to kiss her on the neck while holding both of her breasts in your hands. Caution: don't grab her tits. Mimic the action of the ancient archaic chastity device called the 'Bra.' This device holds the breasts up from the bottom. The upper breasts and especially the nipple are never in play. Engaging the nipples will usually increase the intensity of the Bitch Program instead of exiting out of it. Any time the nipples are touched while the Mark One is in a Bitch Program will result in aggressive behavior from your Help-mate. Remember that the Bitch Program was installed in your Mark One because of demands from many users. They were used to bitch behavior from their mother figure as a child and for one reason or another wished to relive this behavior when feeling lonely. We, of the Design Team, realize that this is not a healthy behavior but we are supplying a service tool; we are not judges; nor do we wish to be.

Our recommendation is that once you start kissing a Mark One, don't ever stop unless the Mark One pulls away. Doing so will only induce feelings of rejection, leaving her open to passing viruses. Especially open, in this case, to the deadly Other Man Virus.

It is not our intention to dissuade you from performing the Restart whenever you feel that your Mark One requires it. Some users perform a Restart every day just to keep their Mark One in tip top condition. This is your option as a user to how you will use your Mark One. We of the Design Team do encourage you to, speaking anthropomorphically again; screw her brains out each and every day to keep your Mark One's CPU in up to standard condition.

DESTRUCTIVE REFORMAT

In the worse case situations, your female might be so ill adjusted and her hard drive may be contaminated with viruses that there will be no other solution than proceeding with a destructive reformat. Do not take this step lightly. After the reformat, your female will be completely without the knowledge or ability to perform in our modern world. Since it will take several days to upload the programs to allow her to act normally, the user must be prepared to forgive his female from any actions or verbal statements that the female might do or say. She is not responsible for her behavior. You are. You initiated the reformat because you allowed your female to become so out of sorts, to use a psychologically kind phrase.

To avoid having to perform a destructive reformat in the first place, it is important to realize that the main purpose of your female is to be used in a Pleasure Program. Failure to activate your females Pleasure Program at least once a week, preferably once a day, will lead to the female becoming more receptive to passing viruses. The most destructive of possible viruses is the "Other Man" virus. Every effort should be made to prevent contamination by this dangerous virus.

Another dangerous virus is the "Freedom" Virus. In this virus the female appears to act as if she is no longer a service creature but a free and independent person. This radical virus is especially destructive to your female. As we all know females are incapable of independent rational thought. Instead they require the guiding hand of a male lifeform to keep her from "Flying off the handle," as the psychologists so quaintly put it. Under the influence of this virus, your female will spend all of her time caring for her children instead of tending to the needs of her user. Obviously every effort should be made to eradicate this virus in all females.

Viruses are most often caught when females gather together in grocery store queues, playground park benches and laundromats. While such locations and their manuals are contained within the female's data banks, the careful user should be sure to limit the female's exposure to such dangerous sites as much as possible.

After a destructive reformat has been preformed, it is necessary to be very sure to dress your female in as sexy clothes as your budget will allow. This is to reinforce the fact that your female is essentially an android built around a Pleasure Program.

With care and foresight a destructive reformat might never have to be preformed, but if it is required, there is every hope of a satisfactory result and a fully functioning female operating within design parameters will be the end result.

Past users have complained that their present female has experienced sexual experiences with other users. This is not possible with a Mark One Help-mate. She will not initiate sexual behavior with another male without your explicit command. In fact as in many android life forms, they will only recognize commands if you repeat the order three times. You must tell your Mark One three times to please your best friend sexually before she will recognize it as a legal order.

This is a big relief to many users. Now they know that if they prefer to keep their Mark One for their own personal use, she will be his only. What a relief! There is something in this world that we can be sure about!

If for some reason you are not sure and wish to proceed with a destructive format but lack the technical know how, the Design Team does hold classes for the technically backwards once a month. Be sure to bring paper, pencils, a Cray adaptable computer or better and, as always, a treat for the teacher.

CHANGING USERS

Changing users with the adult Mark One Female is always a dangerous procedure. Your female has been programmed to treat you, the user, as the only true source data and will ignore all other users. If for one reason or another you feel that you must change females, approach the situation with care. It is especially important to create back ups before proceeding; however it is very possible that you will damage the hard drive by starting the Change User Program and that the female will be of little use afterwards unless you desire a weeping, crying bitch. For some reason the Annoying Program and the Bitch Program never seems to be damaged in this situation. Be aware that your female may even become violent and throw whatever is at hand, some times with deadly accuracy. We of the Design Team are aware of the negative aspects of this situation, however to date we have made little progress creating an easily installed fix. We hope that with the new series which may come out within the next decade or two, this problem will be eradicated. Until then it is best to proceed carefully when changing users.

Interestingly for a time the new user will seem to be very pleased with your old unit, however the damage to the hard drive is extensive and aberrations in behavior will be noticed after time. One of the aberrations is that the female will no longer ignore all other users. If fact in extreme cases the female will pursue other users even in the presence of her official user. You, the old user, may even be sued by the new user for selling damaged goods. Do not fall for this.

The briefest inspection by the new user would have revealed the activated erratic behavior tic on the top right corner of the right eyelid. While the female may learn to control the activation of this tic in order to acquire a new user, running the most basic diagnostic program, accessed through the USB port deep within her belly button, will show the true extent of the damage.

The strangest damage that may occur in the female is that she will believe that she is no longer essentially a helper life form, a servant if you will, and start believing she is in command. She will insist that you the user take her out to dinner and a movie just to activate her Pleasure Program, which after all is one of the female's main purposes. The Design Team is struggling with this problem as well. If the female becomes so erratic that it bothers the user, the best procedure is to de-activate the female and call for removal. Presently procedures are in place to provide for de-activated females in a kind and humane manner. It is cautioned that the user should never download the female's memory bank and try to upload it into another female. A fatal error will always result. Legally the new owner will have no recourse at all and reimbursement is out of the question.

We will not leave you out in the cold as it might be termed, as a past user, you qualify for deep discounts on a new female. We are always there for you!

(Discounts are sometimes as much as .5%)

CHILDBIRTH

Many users have asked about the possibility that their Mark One Female can experience Childbirth. We are glad to confirm that the Mark Two will contain a viable womb and with appropriate test tube technology the Mark Two will be able to give birth to a female 'human' baby. Genetic tendencies of the user will be cloned with Mark capabilities. Unfortunately as of date, despite endless requests, no plans are in the works for a Mark series male able to inject viable sperm. The planning committee is considering many such ideas. Letters should be sent to the Planning Committee, never to the Design Team.

The resultant female born of the Mark One will have many of the personality quirks of the user. It should be realized that the new female will not be totally human, nor will it be a complete Mark One Female. We are creating a new life form. New to us, new to the world.

To avoid endless pain and suffering, the Mark Two Female has access ports to both access the baby and for the eventual birth. Pre birth test are easily done via the usual USB port deep within the Mark Two's belly button.

It is unknown at this time what the legal status of the child will be. The child is not completely human nor is it completely android. It shares the user's DNA and the Mark One's physical capabilities. We have lawyers appearing

before the Congress this year. We would like the offspring
to have full legal rights as a human and as a citizen

FOR ADVANCED USERS

Many users are on their second or third Mark One Female. One must admire their patience. Each time a female is acquired, an exhaustive learning process must take place both on the part of the user and the female. It is far wiser, once one has a female mostly trained, to stay with the female you are used to. If new processes are required, it is much easier to update your female than to acquire a new female with such processes already installed. There are several reasons for this.

I am ashamed to say that all too often highly touted advancements in female technology are sold while they are still in beta. Many companies do this. Microcotton (the name has been changed to protect the Design Team) comes easily to mind. They often release programs that have more problems than benefits. All companies do this to some degree. Ours included. Advancements in technology are expensive. Upper management are always concerned about the bottom line and worry that they might release the most wonderful product but go broke doing so. Not that we accept their excuses.

Your female contains an amazing number of programs, all competing for CPU time. All female users are used to the 'mood' swings females experience as one program or another are allowed to dominate the CPU. One problem is when the female is in a Cooking Program and she is not receiving sufficient attention (or what the female believes to be insufficient attention) the

Bitch Program manages to dominate the CPU and the user not only is not fed but also has to avoid being hit by flying dishes. The only solution to this is to increase the size of the CPU. The Design Team has searched diligently for space in the female's main frame to add additional CPU sub-units and has finally managed to add units in the breast area. Unfortunately, this has increased the breast area which gives the female an unbalanced look. However, the Design Team was surprised to find that many users prefer the 'New Look' over the last model. Obviously the users recognize the advantages of increased CPU size which is why the new units are selling so well.

One problem with the increased CPU size is the female tends to over heat. To cool the unit down, the Design Team changed the color of the protective covering of the main CPU unit in the head. The old brown or black color was changed to a whitish color that the sales department labeled, 'Blonde.' Users also seem to prefer these new models, no doubt because the increased cooling allows the Pleasure Program to dominate CPU usage. Upper management worried that the decreased usage of the Cooking and Cleaning Programs would adversely affect sales; however the new models have remained popular leaving the sales team scratching their heads.

In researching for the most efficient cooling color, the Design Team tested a reddish hue. Even though this color was seen as being more energy efficient than black, the CPU became more erratic. Beta testers labeled the redheaded model, 'Fiery.' This model was released in a limited run and has experienced success with a small percentage of users.

Most advanced users are interested in the orgy sub-routine. Not only will your Mark One act as an initiator of the orgy, but will also be the first to strip off her clothes. She will be the life of the party making sure that none of your friends are left as wall flowers. The Mark One has no restraints on physical endurance. In fact the Mark One can make love from now until the end of time with out stopping for a break.

If the user so requests, the Mark One will hook the user up with whom ever he requests. The Mark One has no jealousy program; she will however ask that the user washes himself thoroughly after any such an orgy. The reason why has not been determined at this time. It is thought that the Mark One at times thinks that she is a human female. The Design Team is trying to eradicate this bug.

MODIFICATION

One of the advantages of the Mark One Female is the female can be modified to suit the demands and desires of the user. Older female models, who have been updated by previous users, are hard wired to perform in ways that may not please the new owner as newer more agile models come on line.

This is not to say that previously owned females are less desirable than one just out of the box. Older models come with many programs already installed, saving the new owner time, money and the frustration of updating their Mark One Female.

Some users insist that they want a model just out of the box as they want a female that has been untouched. This is unrealistic. The user must be aware that every female has been tested before leaving the factory. A little known fact is every female comes with a self testing program installed to reassure the female that she is performing properly. One of the most important self tests is hard wired into the Pleasure Program. Using this test the female can be certain that her circuits are firing properly, even if her user is complaining that she is not interested or not capable of reacting properly.

Another modification is to the Annoying Program. This program is used by users who for one reason or another wish to be belittled by their females. The modification has an emergency stop to the program if the user becomes bored with his female's behavior. The modification requires the user to lay the female over his knees and spank the area between the female's upper thigh and lower back. The user should be aware that this modification will often turn on the Rejection Program. In this program the female will constantly state that she is going back to her mother's. Surprisingly, there is equal chance that this modification will turn on the Pleasure Program, with the female stating,

"About time I got some action around here!"

An interesting modification is an adjustment to the Cleaning Program. Often in your Mark One Female, once the cleaning program has started, your female will ignore all other requests from the user until the program finishes running. The modification allows the user to start the Pleasure Program directly from an unfinished Cleaning program. To initiate the change, the user must twist the Mark One's nipples in the following manner. The right one must be twisted to the right, the left nipple, twisted to the left. Care must be taken not to twist too hard or this will perform a crash of the Cleaning Program and an emergency start of the Bitch Program. This is caused by a virus we have named the 'You Bastard' virus. To date every effort to eradicate this dangerous virus has been unsuccessful. The Design Team has high hopes for the future. Every effort must also be made not to twist the right nipple to the left and the left nipple to the right. Such a command will instruct the female to hibernate. To reinitiate, an expensive visit to the Design Team must be endured.

The Design Team is also struggling to eradicate a 'Trojan Horse' virus that appears only during the play offs. As soon as the user sits down in his easy chair in front of the TV, his Help-mate starts a cleaning program involving vacuuming just the area between the user and the TV. This behavior can only be prevented if the user initiates a Pleasure Program an hour before the game is due to start. Why this virus reacts this way is unknown at this time. Until a fix can be found, the user is advised to be sure to activate the female's Pleasure Program each and every day for a well functioning female irregardless of the schedule of the play offs.

Your female can operate many different programs, but the program that needs the most modification is the Shopping Program. Unless the female receives explicit directions, the Help-mate will bring home vegetables, fruit, tofu and yogurt from the grocery store, completely forgetting chips, beer, hot dogs and rotisserie chicken. The only sure way of making sure your needs are met, is to go to the store with your female. However great success has been achieved by instructing your female to go and get her hair done before going to the supermarket. Why this should make the slightest difference in shopping preference is at present a mystery.

OPTIONS

Your female comes with a full set of options. However, the Design Team encourages you to carefully read the directions before you activate any option sub routine in the control panel. If not carefully followed, once selected, the option can not be deleted. Some options are unfortunately tied to other behaviors. We are trying to erase these ties when we find them, but surprisingly some users seem to like these bizarre behaviors.

For example, if the user selects gourmet cook as an option, the female will insist that the user remove the trash bin in the form of a paper or plastic bag and place it in a receptacle beyond the living quarters of the female dwelling. Some members of the Design Team believe that the female becomes allergic to this trash; others believe that the female is starting to become self aware, much like Hal in the movie 2001, and is trying to establish dominance over the user. Needless to say, we are trying to eradicate this tag along behavior.

Along the same lines, be careful when selecting sexual behavior. For some unknown reason when selecting faithfulness as an option the female seems to feel that the user should be faithful to her, the female. How this association of ideas came about is unknown, some believe it was caused by the 'DoMe1st' virus. The female is essentially an android whose primary function is to act as a sex toy. Granted that the Mark One has become so advanced that the distinction between android and human has become blurred. Some Users have referred to their Mark One as an Advanced Human Woman or as some say, a Mark Two Woman.

An option most users opt for is Masseuse. The only possible problem here is if you select the sub-routine Sexual Massage. There are two further options here: Frontal Massage and Rear Massage. Because these two options are so similar to the Pleasure Program it is easy for the user to become confused. When the Mark One is operating as Masseuse, she will not take part in any sexual behaviors other than massage. The user often, in the throes of passion, becomes confused and believes that his Mark One is faulty when he asks his Help-mate to, in the vernacular, "Screw his brains out." Your Mark One will happily respond to this request when she is in a Pleasure Program, but not in a Masseuse sub-routine. Our advice is to enjoy your massage, consider it as foreplay, and then start the Pleasure Program once the Massage has ended.

If the female is in a Shopping Program, she might be directed to buy Man foods: chips, dogs, chili, and beer. At times the female might well return from the store with lettuce, celery, tofu, milk, and baby food. The user might well complain to the Design Team that his Mark One is faulty. It is not true. In these cases it is always found that the user has not been dominant enough towards the female so she moved into this power vacuum, trying to take over. Females, human or android, will always try to dominate if allowed. The user must always attempt to retain the upper hand when dealing with the female. It is not always easy.

Those users who are unhappy are more than welcome to return their Mark One and try their luck with a human woman instead. We will keep your Mark One in storage while you are engaged in this experiment for a nominal charge.

(Not greater than the original cost.)

REPAIR

The Mark One Female is not easy to repair. Often they exhibit behavior that has nothing to do with the basic problem. When approaching a non-functioning female it is always best to run a full diagnostic starting with the simplest programs and working towards the more advanced. Here is an example of a repair problem.

"Hi, Honey, I'm home."

"It is about time you got home. I have been working my fingers to the bone and do I get any thanks? No! Not a word. At least you could have called and let me know you were worried about me. I could have been laying here dying of lung cancer, but did you think of calling? I don't think you ever think of me unless you want to go to bed, well you can forget about that, buster."

You try again,
"Honey, did you have lunch?"

"Lunch? Lunch? All you think of is your stomach. If you think I am going to make something for you, think again, buster!"

The above responses exhibit a female in dire need of repair. Basic repairs for some unknown reason, at this time, involve applications of blooming plants and sugar laden chocolate. Why food and odor producers should affect the behavior of a presumably rational being is being studied. Other repairs involve shiny articles that are worn on the woman's fingers, neck or ears.

Here is an example of a basic repair.

"Hi, Honey, I'm home. Close your eyes and you might get something nice."

"What did you get me, you wonderful man? Oh, my goodness, how lovely! Come here you sexy creature. I have a present for you. Something that you have always wanted to do!"

More advanced repairs involve, unfortunately, more expensive applications. Eating of expensive food at overpriced soup kitchens, buying of flimsy articles of clothing at very overpriced 'boutiques', and always going to see a cinematic experience before eating at the soup kitchen, are examples of advanced repairs. Surprisingly, the simple bending of the knee and repeating of the meaningless phrase, "I am sorry," seems to function just as well.

The Design Team is continually working on advanced repairs. Sometimes the most basic repairs are the best. Restarting your female should always be tried first by putting her in her charging dock, she will insist on calling it a 'bed'. Often after 8 or more hours of dock time, the female in need of repair will function normally. If that doesn't work, try rebooting by activating a pleasure program. This seems to cancel any aberrations in the female's hard drive. Why it should do so, is being studied. At the present time it is felt that returning the female to one of her main functions is calming to her circuits and hard drive.

Surprisingly, often nothing at all is wrong with your female, even though her Pleasure Program is malfunctioning. This is because she is stuck in a Housework Program as the program has hung up due to a completion error. Make sure that your female has completed her other programs before you activate her Pleasure Program or you will find her unresponsive and her hands making idle, repetitive cleaning motions in the air even while lying in bed on her back.

Needlessly to say, while the female is in 'Dock Time' her personal cleanliness is being tended to. Every Mark One, when she begins a Pleasure Program is in perfectly pristine condition. It would take a masterful eye to realize that she is not in a virgin state.

It should be noted that the Mark One is constructed slightly differently than a woman born of Eve. A Mark One has circular muscles all the way down her throat which allows her to massage your male member in a manner never before experienced. Actually, in a matter of fact, the Mark One is such a valuable item, you really should not share. If you do, your friend will just become filled with thoughts of larceny and desires of theft. Both of which will just require more eventual repairs.

It may be that one day you will notice that your liquor cabinet is becoming emptier faster than normal. This is not un-normal. Your Mark One really wants to think of herself as a human. If she sees you having your nightly aperitif, she will want to have one too. If your do not offer, she will try some on her own.

It doesn't make sense. She is an android. Alcohol cannot influence her one way or the other. It is impossible. She is influenced by electrons only. But something inside or her wants to try. Just once or twice. Just to see. The best thing to do is offer her a drink come cocktail time. Let her join your little celebration. You don't even have to put alcohol in her glass. It doesn't matter one way or the other. You might well see a change in your Mark One.

The truth is she can tell if there is alcohol in her drink. All androids scan anything that enters their bodies. And they do have human flesh. Alcohol can influence her to some small degree. In some models, for an unknown reason, a drink during 'Happy Hour' causes the Mark One to perform her Pleasure Program with increased enthusiasm. Why this is so is being studied.

SECURITY

The security of your female is a very real issue in this increasingly criminal world. Many females, especially newer models, are a target for thieves. A properly trained and updated female is a valuable item and well worth protecting. The following are possible actions you might consider to secure your female.

One of the problems of owning a female is if she is still running a Pleasure Program when you leave her to attend to an emergency at work, and because you did not complete the program, the female might well grab the first user she can find and complete the program to her satisfaction. If you must leave your female because of business matters or important games of golf, make sure your female is in a cleaning or cooking program. That will occupy her for hours if not all day.

Consider also activating the Leash Program which is a sub-routine of all Mark One Females available for a minor pittance from the Design Team. In this program, the female is mentally tied to her dock until her user exits her out of the program. If she is taken away by a third party, she will make every effort to return to her original position. In the meantime, while away, she will be stuck in the Lease Program and will be unable to start any other programs. Out of kindness, the Design Team has allowed her to solve crossword puzzles while she is in Leash. This prevents her from overheating in an endless loop thus destroying delicate circuits.   Another program available for purchase is a variation of the Bitch Program. If the female walks more than 100 feet away from her dock, she immediately starts the Bitch Program. There is a sub-routine that refuses to allow the female to cease the Bitch Program until she is returned to her dock.

The best solution is to always keep your female at your side. For not that much more than you already spent for your Mark One, you are able to update her to a Secretary Program; and for just a pittance more, into an Executive Secretary Program. Now your female can assist you at work and still be your willing female when you return to your home. In fact, by activating the Around the Desk sub-routine, you are able to enjoy your female at work as well. Sub-routines for various sports are available. The Mark One is capable of playing championship golf making her more than capable of winning your endless bets.

"My girl caddie can beat you at this hole with one eye closed!"

"My caddie can beat your caddie using her clubs upside down!"

We wish you to be aware that the purpose of the Mark One is not to win you money but to assist you as a helpful mate. That being said, the Mark Two now in the planning stages has the magnetic ability to break the bank in Las Vegas's One Arm Bandits. Not that we condone such activity. This ability also allows her to open any safe just in case you have forgotten the combination.

The fact that the Mark One cannot be distinguished from a woman born of Eve gives you an extremely powerful edge in the business world. Not only does she have the computing capability and speed of a Cray mainframe, she is capable of acting as a personal body guard. These facts make her a very valuable asset. It behooves you to see to her security. Most users always sleep with their Mark One. Not only can they oversee her security, but she can secure you from any attempt at kidnapping. To avoid any attempt by a third party to hide a listening device on the body of your female, we advise that you always insist that she sleep naked.

The spouses of some users complain about this at first, however as soon as they realize that the Pleasure Program can include them as well and that the tongue of the Mark One exceeds 5 Stars in sex toy ratings, they soon insist that the Mark One sleep in between the very happily married couple.

Aren't you glad you picked a Mark One Female for your Help-mate!

TOOLS

Your Mark One Female is the most amazing tool you will ever buy. Not only does she excel in her patented Pleasure Program which contains all known memories of sirens from Cleopatra to Marilyn Monroe, plus she is completely interactive as only an android can be.

While it is true that the United States Congress is attempting to ban the Mark One Female as fewer children are being born these days, we contest the idea that men's infatuation with the Mark One is causing them to ignore their wives. Unless, that is, the Congress is willing to accede that the American wife is a sexless, personality deficient, drone. Of course, we believe that the American woman excels in love; exceeded perhaps by only French women, and that the Mark One Female simply gives the wife some well deserved relief in bed and in the house work. Many wives have written to us of the Design Team, thanking us for the satisfaction our Mark One has granted them.

The Mark One is an exceptional tool in other ways as well. The alert wife will notice that the Mark One's left canine tooth has a hook in it that works wonderfully as a can opener. Clothes dryers are no longer needed as the Mark One with her servo-powered forearms can wring clothes completely dry in seconds. Cleaning the house is a snap as the Mark One's left eye is digitally enhanced to pick out the smallest piece of dirt and even large microbes thus keeping a completely sanitary house a breeze.

In order for your wife to become the Mark One Female's co-user, you the main user must simply accessing the Mark One's main frame through the USB port in her belly button, punching in the correct series of security codes, identifying your wife with Social Security number, finger print and retinal scan; your wife can become the Mark One's co-user for a specified number of hours a day.

The user's pleasure of relaxing in your recliner as the Mark One obeys your every command must be experienced to be believed. Many wives, when they reach their Sixties, give their husbands a Mark One asking only for co-user rights during weekdays. What husband could refuse? As human women age they do lose some of their sexual desire. Not their fault, it is the way She made them. Why their husband's sexual desire doesn't also decline, is a mystery only She knows.

As a bodyguard, the Mark One Female has no peer. A simple scan of the 'Terminator' movies will give the slightest hint of what an android is capable of. Please note that if you order your Mark One to use a knife to remove the skin on her forearm, it is not covered in your warranty. The biggest advantage of a Mark One is she looks like a Hollywood starlet. No one would expect that she would be capable of demolishing any pugilist with a single blow.

As a best friend, the Mark One excels. If your wife wants to let her hair down with someone, she can't do better than a Mark One. Your Help-mate has an extensive vocabulary of over 200,000 words and her Cray adaptable on board CPU is more that capable of keeping up with your wife's prattling.

As a nanny, the Mark One can teach your son how to throw a curve ball or your daughter the secrets of making and keeping friends and how exactly can you make a bra sexy.

All in all, the best purchase you can or ever will make is a Mark One Female Help-mate. Buy one today. Your life, and your wife, will never be the same again!

Tired of your children coming home with below average grades? The Mark One Female can be your children's homework tutor. Teachers at school don't have time to give your child individual attention. At home your Mark One can. She can explain in easy English what their teacher was trying and failing to describe. For just a few extra dollars your Mark One can be installed with a Teacher Program. Available for all grades up to PhD!

CONCLUSION

As our modern world becomes ever so more complicated, we need help just to keep our heads above the water. That help is here, she is the Mark One Female Help-mate ®™.

No longer does your wife have to work her fingers to the bone, and then return home from work and start over. No longer will you be so grumpy, for your wife will have the energy to take care of your needs. No longer will life be a slow trod to the grave. Now life can be a joy and an adventure like it was always supposed to be. And all because of your brand new Mark One Female!

Your wife will be happy, you will be happy, the kids will have a built in homework tutor, you will be the envy of the neighborhood. So why exactly are you waiting? Heaven's gate is just down at the mall. Jump up out of that chair and change your life!

A Mark One Female, yours for no money down, easy credit, money back for qualified buyers! DO IT!

(Certain restrictions apply)

www.ingramcontent.com/pod-product-compliance
Lightning Source LLC
Chambersburg PA
CBHW060632030426
42337CB00018B/3314